A VERY ASIAN
GUIDE TO
KOREAN FOOD

Written by **MICHELLE LI**
Illustrated by **SUNNU REBECCA CHOI**

What is
KOREAN FOOD?

Korean food is a type of Asian food (and yes, it's *very* Asian), but it is so much more. Korean food has a lot of variety and many flavors. It can be very bold, very spicy, and very fun.

Above all else, it is meant to be shared with others – with friends, family, or even someone you've never met. Take a seat at the table and let's explore Korean food!

#VeryAsian is a celebration of food and culture.

Kaja (가자)
Let's go!

Korean food is so delicious
or mah-sheet-dah (맛있다),
you just can't keep it
to yourself.

KIMCHI / 김치 (KIM-CHEE)

Kimchi is a staple in Korea and is eaten with every meal. It is made of vegetables that are salted, seasoned, and packed in jars to ferment for a few days until the kimchi smells and tastes sour.

The most popular kind of kimchi is red napa cabbage kimchi. It has a spicy kick! Other vegetables like daikon radishes, cucumbers, or chives can be used to make kimchi too.

Kimchi was traditionally made by placing the vegetables in a big pot and burying it underground during winter - nature's refrigerator.

Very Tangy

In the fall, groups of people gather to prepare large jars of kimchi. This is called kimjang. You might have to wear gloves to protect your hands if you are making your kimchi with spicy chili.

Kimchi is so important, some homes have separate refrigerators just for different kinds of kimchi.

Kimchi was first created almost 4,000 years ago.

I'm a kimchi refrigerator

If stored properly, kimchi doesn't go bad, it just ferments more, making it tangier.

Very Shareable

Families make big batches of banchan to eat over several days.

BANCHAN / 반찬 (BON-CHON)

Banchan isn't just one dish – it's many little side dishes served along with every meal. They can vary from kimchi to pickled vegetables, cooked vegetables, savory pancakes, and grilled fish.

You share it with the entire table. At restaurants, waiters constantly refill the dishes so there's always plenty of banchan for everyone.

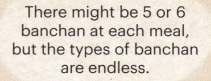

There might be 5 or 6 banchan at each meal, but the types of banchan are endless.

KIMBAP / 김밥 (GEEM-BOP)

Kimbap may look like Japanese sushi, but this Korean seaweed roll is very different. It can be filled with all sorts of ingredients, like spam, fish cake, or bulgogi. Kimbap is rolled up in seaweed and rice with crunchy pickled daikon, spinach, carrots, and egg.

Sometimes people coat day-old kimbap in egg and fry it in a pan.

It's a treat to eat the "messy" ends when the kimbap is sliced up.

Kimbap is a favorite on-the-go snack, perfect for picnics.

This is a kid snack and is often packed for school field trips – most parents send extra kimbap to thank teachers for their hard work.

Snackab!e Very

VERY PLUMP

MANDU / 만두 (MAHN-DOO)

Mandu are dumplings – often filled with vegetables and pork. They can be eaten as a main dish, shared as a side dish, or added as an ingredient in other dishes like soup.

You can cook mandu in many ways - deep-fried, pan-fried, steamed, or boiled.

Many families get together on New Year's and make mandu together.

It's easy to buy frozen mandu in stores, or if you're in Korea, you can find them in "snack restaurants" or bunshik-jip (분식집).

What kinds of foods do you make with your family?

Very Slippery

JAPCHAE / 잡채 (JOP-CHAY)

Japchae is a noodle dish made with a mix of vegetables, meat, and glass noodles. It's usually eaten warm while the noodles are soft and served as banchan, although it can be a main dish too.

Before it's time to cook, people often soak the noodles to make them soft and then cut them with scissors.

The glass noodles, dangmyeon (당면), are made from sweet potato and are see-through.

Japchae is served at nearly every celebration or party.

Very Chewy

TTEOKBOKKI / 떡볶이 (DUCK-BOH-GEE)

Tteokbokki are super chewy rice cakes cooked in a sweet and spicy Korean chili sauce with fish cakes and a boiled egg.

There are lots of versions of tteokbokki, dating hundreds of years back, but red spicy tteokbokki is the most popular today.

Try sprinkling some mozzarella cheese on top, making it extra stretchy, chewy, and gooey.

Serve it with fried vegetables to make a great combo.

It's a popular street food in Korea. You can almost always find tteokbokki stands in front of schools because kids love them as after-school snacks.

Tteokbokki is fun to say and chew.

Or make it a fusion dish by using a creamy alfredo sauce.

It's very tubular.

KOREAN CORNDOGS / 핫도그

Korean corndogs are like none other. They're sold on the streets and are very creative. Sometimes they're coated with cubed French fries or filled with stretchy cheese.

Once the corndogs are fried, they're lightly rolled in sugar, making them sweet and salty.

Korean corndogs can be made with meat, fish cakes, or cheese.

VERY FUN

In Korea, corndogs can be made with just about anything. In fact, the more creative the corndog, the better!

The stretchy mozzarella ones are fun to eat.

What kind of toppings would you put on a corndog?

Very Colorful

BIBIMBAP / 비빔밥 (BEE-BIM-BOP)

Bibimbap means "mixed rice." It's a bowl of rice topped with a variety of cooked vegetables, meat, or tofu, served with a fried egg on top.

It was a traditional farmer's dish. People used to make this dish as a way to use day-old rice and leftovers.

Bibimbap can be served in a hot stone bowl called dolsot (돌솥), which cooks the rice at the bottom, making it very crispy. It's the best part.

Bowls of bibimbap are mixed with a sweet and spicy sauce called gochujang (고추장).

The dish has many ingredients and is all about balance - from colors to flavors.

To eat, mix all the ingredients together so every bite has a bit of everything. You can also mix and match ingredients so every bite is a different adventure.

Very Sweet & Savory

BULGOGI / 불고기 (BUL-GOH-GEE)

Bulgogi means "fire meat" and is one of many kinds of Korean barbecue.

Bulgogi is thinly sliced beef or pork that is first marinated in a sweet and salty sauce made from Asian pear, soy sauce, sesame oil, ginger, and onion and then cooked over a hot grill or pan.

Bulgogi is sometimes used in burgers and tacos to make the ultimate fusion feast.

Bulgogi is an ancient dish that was originally created for royalty.

Very Crispy

KOREAN FRIED CHICKEN / 치킨

Korean Fried Chicken (also called KFC) is a global sensation! It is incredibly crispy because it's double fried and coated in potato starch or tapioca flour. It can be eaten plain, covered in sweet or spicy sauces, or dipped in salt and pepper.

It's been said there are more KFC stands in Korea than McDonald's and Subways around the world.

It's always served with a refreshing side of crunchy pickled radishes.

Many Korean dramas feature KFC on their shows, making it even more popular across the globe.

It's crispy, crunchy, and crackly.

Very Hot

SUNDUBU JJIGAE / 순두부찌개 (SOON-DOO-BOO JEE-GAY)

Sundubu jjigae is a hot, spicy, and velvety stew made with extra soft tofu, vegetables, and sometimes meat or seafood. It's one of the most popular stews in Korea because it's so filling, so flavorful, and so hot.

It is eaten with a bowl of rice.

순두부

Sundubu jjigae becomes spicy and red thanks to a spice called gochugaru (고춧가루), Korean red pepper flakes.

It's fun to add a raw egg and watch it cook.

It's served bubbling hot, making it a great wintertime stew to keep you warm on a cold day.

TTEOKGUK / 떡국 (DUCK-GOOK)

Tteokguk is a brothy soup filled with disk-shaped rice cakes. Tteokguk is usually garnished with thinly-sliced cooked eggs, marinated meat, and seaweed.

People eat it on Seollal (설날), Korean New Year, which is the first day of the Lunar calendar. It's usually eaten for good luck.

Eating tteokguk on New Year's marks getting older by one more year – almost like it's everyone's birthday. But you can also eat tteokguk any day.

VERY Traditional

A lot of people celebrate two New Year's days - January 1 and Lunar New Year - and eat tteokguk on both.

It's best to eat right away so the rice cakes don't get mushy.

The disk-shaped rice cakes symbolize coins and prosperity.

Very Refreshing

BINGSU / 빙수 (BING-SOO)

Bingsu is Korean shaved ice topped with chopped fruit, pieces of rice cake, and sweet red bean, with a layer of condensed milk at the bottom. It's a traditional dish that is still very popular today.

Milk can be frozen instead of water, making creamy milk ice that melts faster in your mouth.

It's one of the most popular summer desserts.

Sweetened red beans are found in many Korean desserts - they're boiled and mixed with sugar and vanilla. Mini rice cakes add a nice chewy texture to each bite. Bingsu is sometimes topped with cereal for a crunchy and icy bite.

Would you like to eat the goodies at the top or slurp the sweet milky puddle at the bottom?

Very Gooey

HOTTEOK / 호떡 (HO-DUCK)

Hotteok is a sweet dessert pancake that's irresistible. Children especially love this street snack.
The dough is filled with a paste of brown sugar, cinnamon, and chopped nuts. It is then pan-fried until the center melts into gooey goodness.

Serve up the hot pancakes with a glass of milk.

Sometimes peanuts and sesame seeds are added inside, and savory pancakes with kimchi are popular too.

As the pancake heats up in the pan, the cinnamon-sugar paste turns into warm sweet syrup.

Thanks to K-pop,
Korean dramas,
movies, and more.

Korean cuisine is very popular around the world. It's eaten in homes, at restaurants, on trucks, on streets... and brings people together everywhere.

I was inspired to write this book for my family, especially for my son JJ, my husband Jim, and my sister Hyun Jung. My family's heritage comes from a variety of places – Korea, Poland, the Netherlands, and more. While we don't always get to travel to all these places, we can learn about these cultures through delicious food.

Sharing a meal is about adventure, happiness, comfort, and love. I am proud of the very Asian food we make for each other – it's a way we can bring our full humanity to the table while finding respect and admiration for others. I hope that this book is one way I can share with you the many food memories my family and I cherish.

Michelle Li

Michelle's Mandu Recipe

Mandu ingredients:

- 1/2 pound of ground beef (or substitute with tofu)
- 1/4 pound of ground pork (or substitute with tofu)
- 1 small zucchini
- 1 egg
- 1/2 yellow onion, finely chopped
- 2-3 cloves of garlic, minced
- 1 tablespoon of sesame oil
- 1 package of wonton wrappers or mandu skins
- salt
- ground black pepper
- 3-5 pieces of kimchi, minced (optional)
- vegetable oil (or other oil for frying)

Dipping sauce ingredients:

- 2 tablespoons of soy sauce
- 1 tablespoon of rice vinegar
- 2 teaspoons of gochugaru
- 1 scallion

Directions:

- Combine the ground beef, ground pork, egg, onion, and garlic into a large mixing bowl.

- Cut the zucchini into small cubes (about the size of a pencil eraser or smaller) and sprinkle salt on top.

- Place the cut zucchini on a paper towel to absorb the water from the zucchini. Press the zucchini with paper towels to absorb as much moisture from the zucchini. Then, add the zucchini to the rest of the ingredients.

- Add sesame oil, and salt and pepper to taste. Add kimchi. Mix well.

- To fill the dumplings, place a small spoon of filling in the center of the mandu skin (or wonton wrapper). Use your finger to apply a little water on the edge to help seal the dumpling. Fold the skin in half over the filling and press the edges together to make a moon shape or a triangle (depending on the shape of the wrapper). Make tiny pleats where the skins are folded together.

- To steam the mandu, bring a small amount of water to a boil in a large pot. Make sure your steamer is above the water. Place a layer of dumplings inside without touching each other. You can use a bamboo steamer or a regular steamer lined with cheese cloth or similar liner. Cover and steam for about 5 minutes.

- To pan fry the mandu, heat the pan on medium high heat with a couple tablespoons of vegetable oil. Work in batches to add a handful of dumplings in a single layer. Cook until the dumplings are brown on one side, about 3-4 minutes. Add a couple tablespoons of water to the pan to create steam. Turn the heat down to medium low and cover with a lid. Once the water has mostly evaporated, remove the lid and continue cooking for another minute or two until the bottom of the dumplings have become crispy.

Meok-ja! (먹자)

To my two Jims and my loving family. Especially my mom, Sharon, who proved you really can be born in someone's heart – M.L.

To Rosa, Don and Jack – S.R.C.

A Very Asian Guide to Korean Food is first published by Gloo Books 2022
Written by Michelle Li
Illustrated by Sunnu Rebecca Choi
The illustrations in this book were rendered in a mix of acrylic, watercolor, crayon and digital medium.
Text copyright © 2022 Michelle Li
Illustrations copyright © 2022 Gloo Books

For more information or to order books, please visit www.gloobooks.com or contact us at contact@gloobooks.com.

ISBN: 978-1-7372404-2-6

Printed in Canada.
This book was printed on paper certified according to the standards of the FSC®.

FSC
www.fsc.org

MIX
Paper from
responsible sources
FSC® C016245